Treasure Hunt Florence

Ellen and Marvin
Mouchawar

Kids Go Europe™ is a family-oriented company dedicated to helping children learn and enjoy the world.

Copyright © 2006 by Kids Go Europe, Inc.

All rights reserved. No part of this book may be reproduced or transmitted in any form or by any means, electronic or mechanical, including photocopying and recording, or by any information storage and retrieval system, except as may be expressly permitted by the 1976 Copyright Act or by the publisher. Requests for permission should be made in writing to:

Kids Go Europe, Inc.
PO Box 4014
Menlo Park, CA 94026 USA
info@kidsgoeurope.com

Every effort has been made to trace accurate ownership of copyrighted text and visual material used in this book. Errors or omissions will be corrected in subsequent editions, provided notification is sent to the publisher.

ISBN 0-9772699-1-4

Printed in Malaysia

ACKNOWLEDGMENTS
A special thanks to Elaine Ruffolo, Syracuse University Professor and art historian, for her wealth of knowledge and creative insight.

Let's take an adventure
Amongst magical sites
Florentine history
Is sure to excite!

You'll go on a hunt
Not found in your books
To uncover treasures
Sometimes overlooked.

Greet folks with "Buon Giorno"
Rub the nose of a boar
Count medieval towers
Visit the rich and the poor.

Meet the "David" of legends
Who killed a giant with one stone
Climb up the Cathedral
To the top of the dome.

So, let's discover Firenze
As you wander, keep score
The wonders of Florence
Are just out your door.

This Treasure Hunt
Was Undertaken

By: _____
(Hunter's Name)

On: _____
(Date)

NOTE TO GROWN-UPS:

Florence is a city bursting with history and beauty, a city worthy of intense exploration and contemplation. Any guidebook will contain an overwhelming list of "must sees" – the Accademia, the Duomo, the Uffizi, to name just a few – many of which will have long lines depending on when you come. How do you even touch on the highlights with your children in toe; how do you include your children in a meaningful and enjoyable visit to this marvelous city? In the pages that follow, we have attempted to provide you with the tools to do just that! It is our hope that this treasure hunt will enable you to discover Florence as a family, incorporating the remarkable culture, history and magic this incredible city has to offer us all.

We have tried to include most of the important Florentine sites. We have also included some of our favorite treasures not always highlighted in the guidebooks. But this is not an exhaustive study. We purposefully have not included detailed information regarding each question and point of interest. Additionally, we have included no general tourist information. A good tourist guidebook is invaluable in visiting any foreign country. However, that's for the grown-ups to study! Don't defeat your children's curiosity with detailed explanations. They'll wish to hunt for the treasures themselves. So, with a little guidance from us, let them!

Although we have organized the hunt in some semblance of order, feel free to **customize the hunt** to suit your interests, time and the ages of your children. Warning: Do not force yourself beyond reason to do everything! This will only exhaust and frustrate your entire family. Now that we live in Florence with our 9 and 11 year old children, we realize that it would take our family years to uncover all of the treasures hidden herein. Don't rush your way through; if you feel you've missed something, you'll just have to come back.

Finally, we've included several questions specifically for the grown-ups. Players, maybe you can think of other stumpers for them along the way!

The Hunt Begins...

Treasure Hunt Rules 8

Specific Spots Around Town 11

Piazza della Signoria 12
Palazzo Vecchio. 17
Uffizi 18
Museo di Storia della Scienze 27
Bargello 28
Orsanmichele 32
Piazza del Duomo. 33
Duomo. 34
Battistero 36
Museo del Duomo 38
Accademia 42
San Marco 46
San Lorenzo 47
Palazzo Medici-Riccardi 52
Santa Maria Novella 55
Mercato Nuovo 59
Palazzo Davanzati 60
Chiesa di Santi Apostoli 64
Ponte Vecchio. 67
Palazzo Pitti and Boboli Gardens 69
Santo Spirito 74
Santa Croce 75
Piazzale Michelangelo. 76

Questions for Anytime 79

Answers and Interesting Tidbits . . 99

Scorecard 111

The *Florin of Florence*, first gold coin of Western Europe, minted in 1252

Treasure Hunt Rules

This one-of-a-kind game was **created for YOU** to discover the treasures of Florence. If you are playing with siblings or friends, remember: This is a **COOPERATIVE** effort, NOT a competition! You are allowed to – and are supposed to – help each other. Official "Scorekeeper" (ie. your parents/guardians) has the discretion to award points for team sportsmanship.

You will want to breeze through all the questions before you begin (especially those in the last section, *Questions for Anytime*) so that you have all of them in mind throughout the hunt. Points need not be earned in the same order that we put the questions here.

Scorekeeping*

- Keep score on the scorecard supplied on page 111. (Tally marks work best.)
- When you earn **60 points**, AND you all need a break, stop for a treat, BUT it must be an authentic Italian treat.
- When you earn **120 points**, look for a souvenir, which will help you remember your adventure. (Euro limit to be determined by Scorekeeper.)
- When you earn **200 points** (or get kinda close), AND you all need a snack, stop in a nearby bar or cafe and get a *panino* of your choice.
- When you earn **300 points** (give or take a few), you decide the next outing – one veto permitted by the Scorekeeper.

  * Scorekeeper has discretion to alter prizes.

Now, go uncover the treasures of Florence!

Buona Fortuna!

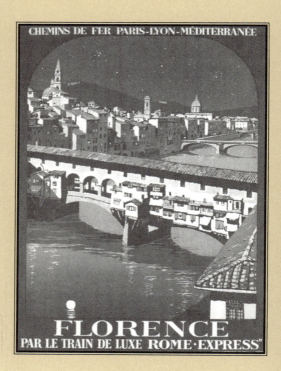

Specific Spots Around Town

Piazza della Signoria

Stand in the center of *Piazza della Signoria*, the heart of Florence, and slowly turn around. Name three things that catch your eye.

2 points each

Piazza della Signoria

Walk over to the immense bronze statue of a man on horseback. Who is he?

2 points

Piazza della Signoria

<u>Challenge to Scorekeeper</u>: It is in this *Piazza* where the "Bonfire of the Vanities" took place. What was it?

Piazza della Signoria

In the *Loggia dei Lanzi*, have your photo taken in front of your favorite statue. Which one did you choose and why?

2 points

Piazza della Signoria

Palazzo Vecchio

Enter the *Palazzo Vecchio* (The "Old Palace"), and find your way to the Room of Maps. List the names of the places you recognize.

1 point each

NOTE: This is known as The "Old Palace," because the Medici moved from here to the *Palazzo Pitti* - possibly because this was just too small?

Uffizi

<u>Challenge for Scorekeeper</u>: What was
the original function of the *Uffizi*?

Uffizi

Find the portraits of the Duke and Duchess of Urbino. Look closely at the Duke. Do you notice something strange about his face?

4 points

Uffizi

Do not miss the room with two of the most famous paintings in the world, "The Birth of Venus" ("*Nascita di Venire*") and "Spring" (or "*Primavera*"). We promise you that these two paintings will capture your imagination. If you are lucky enough to be there when it's not too crowded, take a seat where you can relax and get a good look at these paintings. What grabs your attention? (You might even sketch something that particularly interests you.)

10 points

These paintings hung in one of the Medici's <u>extra</u> bedrooms. Imagine having a sleepover at their house?!

Uffizi

More room for your thoughts:

By the way, what type of fruit trees do you think are in the *Primavera*? (NOTE: No one knows for sure.)

2 points

Uffizi

Find the wall on which three paintings by Leonardo da Vinci hang. The middle painting of Leonardo da Vinci is not finished. What colors would you use if you were painting this picture?

5 points

NOTE: This is the only place in the world that you can see three of his paintings hanging next to each other. It's a great way to see how his style changed over time.

Uffizi

Bonus: In the *Sala di Michelangelo*, you can see Michelangelo's *Doni Tondo*. What is so special about this painting?

3 points

Uffizi

Only if you are not easily frightened, enter
Room 43. Mr. Caravaggio painted some
pretty creepy stuff. How do you feel about
his paintings?

4 points

Uffizi

Bonus: Who was Medusa?

3 points

Some believe that Caravaggio's painting of Medusa is a self-portrait. What do you think of that?!

Uffizi

Can you find the portrait that Mr.
Rembrandt painted of himself as a young
man?

3 points

Museo di Storia della Scienze

Visit the *Museo di Storia della Scienze di Firenze* (Florence's History of Science Museum), where you can see the inventions of Italy's most famous scientists. Describe one of Galileo's inventions.

4 points

Bargello

You're now in the *Bargello*, Florence's
sculpture museum. In the late 1400s,
there was a competition to decide who
would make the doors of the Baptistry.
Seven artists submitted door panels. Find
the competition door panels of the two
finalists. Which one would you have
chosen. Why?

8 points

Bargello

In the same room as the competition panels be sure to check out Donatello's <u>bronze</u> "David." You will want to remember it for a later question (see page 92). You may want to write down some of your impressions here.

3 points

Bargello

<u>Bonus</u>: Donatello also sculpted a "David" out of <u>marble</u>, which stands in the same room as his bronze "David." How are these statues different? How are they similar?

3 points

Bargello

One of the towers of the original Roman
wall that enclosed the city stood right in
front of where the *Bargello* now stands.
The point where it stood has been marked
with a big circle. Can you find it?

2 points

Orsanmichele

Enter the church of *Orsanmichele*. The building's original purpose was an open air grain market. You can still see evidence of its original purpose. Can you find it?

4 points

Piazza del Duomo

As you enter the *Piazza del Duomo* (or "Cathedral Square"), point out:
(1) the *Cattedrale di Santa Maria del Fiore*,
(2) the *Battistero di San Giovanni*, and
(3) the *Campanile di Giotto*.

3 points (total)

Duomo

Enter the *Cattedrale di Santa Maria del Fiore* (the "*Duomo*"), and climb up the inside of Brunelleschi's dome. What do you think of Brunelleschi's amazing accomplishment?

6 points

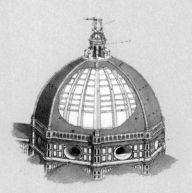

NOTE: This dome is still one of the five highest domes in the world.

Duomo

From the marble lantern at the top of the dome, enjoy the view. What does Florence look like from this height?

5 points

Battistero

Walk into one of the oldest buildings in Florence, the *Battistero* (the "Baptistry"), and stand in the center where every child in Florence used to be baptized. This was the only way to become a Florentine citizen.

3 points

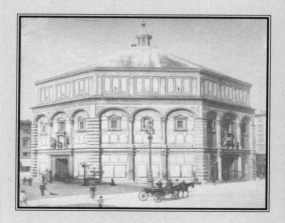

Battistero

Get your photo taken in front of the "Gates of Paradise." (You have to find them first!)

2 points

Museo del Duomo

<u>Bonus</u>: Go see the original "Gates" in the *Museo dell' Opera del Duomo.* (They were just cleaned; so they're pretty amazing!)

5 points

Museo del Duomo

Find the index finger of John the Baptist.
(I'm not kidding!) Do you think it's real?

2 points

Museo del Duomo

In the same room as the finger, check out Donatello's wooden statue of Mary Magdalen. (Imagine: This was carved from a single tree trunk.) Look into the woman's eyes. How do you think she feels?

5 points

Museo del Duomo

<u>Challenge for Scorekeeper</u>: Go to
the room containing the two original choir
lofts by Donatello and Luca della Robbia.
What truly momentous thing occurred in
this room approximately 500 years ago?

Accademia

Visit the *Galleria dell'Accademia*, where you will see the most famous statue in the world, Michelangelo's "David." Slowly walk around it viewing the statue from every angle. Then walk back toward the museum entrance, turn and look at it from afar. Now, write down at least 3 things that you notice about the statue.

8 points (total)

Accademia

More room for your thoughts:

<u>Challenge for Scorekeeper</u>: Who was "David"?

Accademia

<u>Bonus</u>: If you've got the time to linger here, take a seat (if it's not too crowded) and sketch the "David."

10 points

Accademia

Where did Michelangelo's "David" originally stand?

2 points

San Marco

Visit the *Museo San Marco* where you can go into the *Monastero di San Marco*. Head upstairs. Walk down the hallways and go into one of the rooms, called "cells." If you were a Dominican monk back in the 1400s, one of these rooms would be your home. It might have a small bed, a desk and a chair. How does this room compare to your room at home?

5 points

San Lorenzo

Enter the *Basilica di San Lorenzo*. Whose private "family church" was this?

3 points

San Lorenzo

<u>Bonus</u>: Can you find where Cosimo de' Medici, the patriarch of this family, is buried?

2 points

San Lorenzo

You may want to take the time, to wander into the Laurentian Library. Who designed this for the Medici?

2 points

San Lorenzo

Go to the *Mercato di San Lorenzo* and
ask one of the merchants to show you
the team shirt of Florence's soccer team,
"*Fiorentina.*" What does it look like?

2 points

San Lorenzo

What do you do at the *Mercato Centrale*
(the "Central Market")?

2 points

Palazzo Medici-Riccardi

Visit the *Palazzo Medici-Riccardi*, the home of the Medici family throughout the Renaissance. Off the inner courtyard, follow the Virtual Tour of *Capella dei Magi*.

5 points

Palazzo Medici-Riccardi

After following the "virtual tour," head upstairs to the private chapel of the Medici, *Capella dei Magi*. Can you now point out three of the most important men in the Medici family: Cosimo the Elder, Piero the Gouty and Lorenzo the Magnificent?

2 points each

Palazzo Medici-Riccardi

Make your way to the *Sala Luca Giordano*.
On the walls and ceiling, how many
different kinds of animals do you see?
What are they?

I point each

Santa Maria Novella

Looking at the façade (the front) of the *Basilica di Santa Maria Novella*, list all the shapes you see.

3 points (total)

Santa Maria Novella

Santa Maria Novella

Enter the church, and find the *Trinità* (or "Trinity") painted by Mossacio. After the fresco was finished, Florentines flooded this church to view it. Art experts believe that this fresco inspired many great artists, including Michelangelo, who worked in this church as an artist's assistant when he was a young boy. Why do you think this painting is thought to be so special?

6 points

Santa Maria Novella

Around the corner from the *Basilica di Santa Maria Novella*, visit the 14th century pharmacy, still famous all over Europe. The *Officina Profuma-Farmaceutica di Santa Maria Novella*. Wind your way through to the *erboristeria* (the herbalist's shop). Describe the smell.

4 points

Does this look like any pharmacy you've ever been in?!

Walk by the *Mercato Nuovo* (the New Market – it was new in 1551!), and rub the snout of the bronze *Porcellino* fountain. Florentines say this gives you good luck.

2 points

Palazzo Davanzati

Take your time wandering through the
Palazzo Davanzati, where you get a glimpse
into how wealthy Florentines (other than
the Medici) lived in the early 1300s.

2 points

NOTE: Entry is free, there are rarely any lines, and
it has one of the best public bathrooms in Florence.

Palazzo Davanzati

When you first enter the *Palazzo*, look at
the holes in the ceiling. What do you think
these were for? (When you go upstairs
into the main living room, you will see the
top of the holes with hooks on them.)

3 points

Palazzo Davanzati

Go upstairs and wander through the rooms. Find the original bathroom of the *Palazzo*. It was extremely rare for a house to have a bathroom at that time. This would only be found in the houses of the truly rich. What would you think about going to the bathroom here?

3 points

Palazzo Davanzati

Just before you leave, check out the
painting on your left in the entrance hall,
titled "*Storia di Susanna.*" This is a great
way to see how people dressed almost
600 years ago. What are some of the
differences you notice from how people
dress now?

5 points

Chiesa di Santi Apostoli

Visit the *Chiesa di Santi Apostoli* (the
"Church of the Holy Apostles"). If no
one is there, the church will likely be dark
when you walk in. Find your way to a
seat in the middle of the church. Have
the Scorekeeper go to the light box to
the left of the front door, and turn on the
lights. When the lights come on, behold
the treasures of this 1000 year old church.
Look all around you. What do you see?

6 points

Chiesa di Santi Apostoli

More room for your thoughts:

This is one of our favorite spots; it is a great place to take a break and relax for a bit. Entry is free, and you may have the church all to yourselves. (But when you go, have a couple one Euro coins so you can turn on the lights.)

Chiesa di Santi Apostoli

Bonus: Outside the *Chiesa di Santi Apostoli*, find on a wall of the *Piazza del Limbo* a tiny plaque, which shows you how high the river came during the 1966 Florence flood. Was it over your head?

2 points

Ponte Vecchio

Walk across the *Ponte Vecchio*, the oldest of Florence's bridges and one of the most famous landmarks of Florence, where gold merchants have clustered for centuries. Be sure to stop halfway, and take in the view.

2 points

Ponte Vecchio

<u>Challenge to Scorekeeper</u>: What was
the original purpose of this bridge?

Palazzo Pitti and Boboli Gardens

On to the magnificent *Palazzo Pitti*, Florence's largest palace. Wander through the *Galleria Palatina*. As you go, count the rooms of these royal apartments where princes, grand dukes and duchesses lived for 300 years. Keep a tally here. The walls are filled with the Medici's private art collection, and the rooms look much like they would have when they lived here.

3 points

As you enter the *Galleria Palatina*, peek out the windows on the right to catch a glimpse of the Boboli Gardens. You'll have a chance to run around there later.

Palazzo Pitti and Boboli Gardens

Make your way to the *Sala di Saturno*
("Saturn Room") where you will
see Raphael's *Madonna della Seggiola*
("Madonna of the Chair"). Some art
experts say that this painting is "perfect,"
and that after Raphael died, no artist
matched him. What do you think?

5 points

Palazzo Pitti and Boboli Gardens

In the *Musei degli Argenti*, make your way
to the *Sala degli Avori*. Find the Medici
collection of *Vasi Torniti* ("turned vases").
Which is your favorite? Sketch it here.

6 points

NOTE: Each one of these vases was carved from a
single elephant tusk.

Palazzo Pitti and Boboli Gardens

If you have the time, head to the Costume
Gallery, where you can see clothes worn
by people 500 years ago. What would you
have worn if you lived way back then?

3 points

Palazzo Pitti and Boboli Gardens

Spend your time wandering (or running) through the Boboli Gardens. This is a great place to hang out if you need to release some energy. Have your photo taken in front of your favorite statue.

2 points

Santo Spirito

Visit the *Basilica di Santo Spirito*. As you walk around, note what sounds you hear.

3 points

Santa Croce

Visit the *Basilica di Santa Croce*. Name
three of the famous people buried here.

3 points (total)

Piazzale Michelangelo

If you have the time and energy, hike up to *Piazzale Michelangelo*, and take in the panoramic view of Florence. (It's well worth the time and effort!) List all of the landmarks that you recognize.

1 point each

Piazzale Michelangelo

<u>Bonus:</u> Climb even further up to *San Miniato al Monte* and take a peek inside. Did you find any treasures here? What were they?

3 points

Questions for Anytime

Questions to be countered at *Anytime* during your Hunt — when you're waiting in line, bored, or just want to earn some extra points!

Say "*Buon Giorno*" to three people you pass on the street. (If it's after 6:00 pm, say "*Buona Sera*.") What were their responses?

3 points each

Below, draw a picture of the Italian flag.
What colors are on it?

3 points

What body of water splits Florence in half?

2 points

What does the word "Renaissance" mean?

3 points

As you wander through the streets of Florence, count and record the number of towers ("*torre*") you see. (You'll need to look up, but watch out for dog poop!).

1 point each

HINT: There are a number of towers right around the Ponte Vecchio. Many are marked by a historical monument sign.

You will see the coat of arms of the all-powerful Medici all over Florence. (In particular, you can see it all over the *Basilica di San Marco* and the *Palazzo Medici-Riccardi*). Find it and draw the coat of arms here.

5 points

<u>Bonus</u>: Count the number of times you encounter the Medici name.

1 point each (20 points maximum)

Sometime when you need a break, pop into a bar, and order a *cioccolato caldo*. (One particularly famous place is the *Rivoire Cafe Pasticceria* on the *Piazza della Signoria*.) Take a taste. How does this compare to your hot chocolate at home?

3 points

When you visited the Museo del Duomo, you found the index finger of John the Baptist. If you can believe it, Florentines have preserved another finger of a famous person. Who is it?

2 points

How did the Medici walk between their house (the *Palazzo Pitti*) and their offices (the *Uffizi*) and then on to the *Palazzo Vecchio* without having to go outside?

4 points

If you were a local Florentine, you might do your daily shopping in the *alimentari, macelleria, pescheria, salumeria, panetteria, farmacia and cartoleria*. Where would you be going?

3 points each

Remember back to when you visited Donatello's bronze "David" in the Bargello and Michelangelo's "David" in the Accademia. Now, compare the two. What are their similarities? Differences?

10 points

Go to a store where traditional Florentine paper is made. How do they make this beautiful paper?

6 points

HINT: Look in the back of one of the many small stores that sell paper; the workshop is often there. One example (as of Feb. 2006): *Legatoria di Libri, S.Agostina, Via S.Agostina* 21r (near *Santo Spirito*).

As you wander the streets of Florence, find a church not pointed out by one of the grown-ups. Go ahead and peek inside. What was the church? What treasures did you find?

8 points

In this treasure hunt, you should have used all five senses – sight, hearing, smell, touch and taste. Did you? How?

3 points

As you leave Florence, while you're sitting on the train or airplane, think back on your adventure. What are the most memorable treasures you uncovered in Florence?

10 points (Write us and let us know!)

Michelangelo Buonarroti

Answers and Interesting Tidbits

Beware: Once you check out the answers, you can't earn the points!

NOTE: Most questions have no <u>one</u> right answer. However, for those that do, we have included the answers on the pages that follow.

Specific Spots Around Town

Page 13: Cosimo I de' Medici was the first Grand Duke of Tuscany. The Medici was the most powerful and wealthiest family in the history of Florence. For three hundred years, the House of Medici ruled Florence at a time when the city was one of the most important cities in the world. They were one of the primary originators of our modern banking system. They controlled European politics, the great scientists and artists, and even popes. You will encounter the Medici throughout your hunt. They lived in the palaces, they built the churches and they paid for much of the art you will see.

Page 14: In the late 1400s, the colorful and retched character, Dominican Friar Girolamo Savonarola, took it upon himself to cleanse Florence of its sins. He ordered that all personal items of "vanity" – jewels, art, books, musical instruments – be brought to either the *Piazza della Signoria* or the *Piazza San Marco*, and burned in huge bonfires built to purge the city of evil. It is horrifying to think what was destroyed during this purging!

Page 18: These were the offices of the Medici, from where they controlled all of Tuscany. *Uffizi* translates to "offices."

Page 19: Check out the bridge of his nose! In a duel, the Duke lost hearing in his right ear and sight in his right eye. Legend has it that he had the bridge of his nose carved out so that he could see better with his left eye. Now that's gross!

Page 23: There are many answers to this question. One thing to note is that this is Michelangelo's only painting in Florence.

Page 25: According to Roman myth, Medusa was a beautiful woman who, when attacked by the god Poseidon, turned into a horrible monster. She had snakes for hair, and could turn anyone into stone who made the mistake of looking into her eyes.

Page 26: Rembrandt's "Self Portrait as a Young Man" is located in Room 44 - 17th Century Flemish Painters.

Page 32: In the bottom of the left piers and in the rear left corner of the ceiling, you can still see openings which served as shoots where the grain was brought down from the second floor. Additionally, you can see rings in the ceiling, which were originally used as pulleys and to hang lanterns.

Page 41: Michelangelo carved the "David" right here.

Page 43: "David" is the symbol of Florence. The story goes that he was a young boy who, with only rocks and a slingshot, goes out to slay the giant, Goliath. He kills the giant and then cuts off his head. "David" represents the victory of good over evil, young over old, the weak over the mighty, the republic over tyranny. This is why he was chosen as Florence's symbol when Florence became a republic.

Page 45: Michelangelo's "David" originally stood in front of the *Palazzo Vecchio* in *Piazza della Signoria*. In 1873, it was moved to this building, which was built specifically for it.

Page 47: The Medici, of course!

Page 48: Cosimo de' Medici is buried in the crypt below the floor in front of the main altar.

Page 49: Michelangelo designed the Laurentian Library for the Medici.

Page 51: The *Mercato Centrale* is a large food market.

Page 54: On our first trip, we found horses, bulls, a goat, peacocks, foxes, wolves, dogs (including a 3-headed one), tiger, snake, elephant, wild boar, lion, eagle, leopard and -- don't miss the owl. If you find any others, be sure to let us know!

Page 61: These holes were used to pull up supplies and for defense. When the family's enemies made it through the outer doors of the *Palazzo*, someone would drop boiling oil or water onto the intruders' heads. Yikes!

Page 68: The *Ponte Vecchio* was originally the site of Florence's meat and fish market. Butchers, fishmongers, and tanners would gather here to sell their products, throwing the animals' remains into the Arno. It was certainly a dirty and smelly place!

Page 74: As in all churches, you are supposed to be quiet. But in this church, they seem to be especially strict. It should be absolutely silent. Is it?

Page 75: Among others, Michelangelo, Galileo Galilei, Lorenzo Ghiberti and Dante are all buried here. Note: Dante is not actually buried here; his bones rest in Ravenna, and this monument was not erected until 500 years after he died.

Questions for Anytime

Page 82: The River Arno splits Florence in half.

Page 83: The word "Renaissance" means "rebirth." It is the name given to a time when the world's great artists (Michelangelo), writers (Dante), architects (Brunelleschi) and scientists (Leonardo da Vinci) looked back and studied the amazing teachings of the classical Greeks and Romans. It refers roughly to the period during the 15th and 16th centuries.

Page 84: Although sometimes hard to find, towers are all over Florence. People built their homes like this for protection during the dark years of the Middle Ages. *Palazzo Vecchio* has the tallest tower. It was built to house the city government, which wished to dominate Florence's wealthy families – all of whom had tall tower houses. To ensure that *Palazzo Vecchio* remained the tallest tower in Florence, the city rulers decided that no private towers could be taller than 30 meters. Any tower that was taller had to be lowered. At one time, very rich families had towers as high as 60 meters. In searching for towers around the city, you will be getting a glimpse into life in medieval Florence.

Page 88: The middle finger of Galileo Galilei is on display in the History of Science Museum.

Page 89: The Vasari Corridor, one kilometer long, runs from the *Palazzo Pitti* over the *Ponte Vecchio* and all the way to the *Palazzo Vecchio*.

Page 90: *Alimentari* = general grocer's shop (small food store); *macelleria* = butcher shop; *pescheria* = fishery; *salumeria* = deli; *panetteria* = bakery; *farmacia* = pharmacy; *cartoleria* = stationary store (where many Italian children buy their school supplies).

We hope you enjoyed this hunt as you uncovered the treasures of Florence.

Visit **www.KidsGoEurope.com**. We welcome your comments, and in fact, ask that you take the time to let us know what you thought about this treasure hunt. We will listen to you, and you may see your comments incorporated into future treasure hunts.

We plan to make treasure hunts for cities all over Europe – and someday, the world. Where else would you like to go on a treasure hunt??

YOUR NAME COULD BE KNOWN ALL OVER THE WORLD!

How did you do? Record your total point score at www.KidsGoEurope.com and we will post your first name, nationality, age and score. You may become *Il Cacciatore Suprema* (the "Supreme Hunter") for the envy of all fellow hunters across the world.

Be sure to undertake our other treasure hunt:

Kids Go Europe: Treasure Hunt Venice

www.KidsGoEurope.com

Scorecard

ORDER PAGE

To order additional copies, please visit our website

www.KidsGoEurope.com

Or complete and mail the below form to:

Kids Go Europe, Inc.
PO Box 4014
Menlo Park, CA 94026 USA

Please send me:

____copy/copies of **Treasure Hunt Florence**
____copy/copies of **Treasure Hunt Venice**

at $9.95 / copy.   Plus shipping and handling.

Name: _____
Address: _____
City:_____ Prov/State: _____ Zip: _____
Country:_____Telephone: _____
Email: _____

Sales Tax: Please add 7.75% for shipments to California addresses.

Shipping/Handling: Please add $6.00 for first book and $3.00 for each additional copy.

Payment: ___ Check ____ Credit Card

____ Visa ____ MasterCard

Card number: _____
Name on card: _____ Exp date: _____